Bagriy & Co.

GARI LIGHT

CONFLUENCES

COLLECTION OF POEMS

Bagriy & Company
Chicago
2020

ISBN: 978-1-7344460-0-5
Library of Congress Control Number: 2019957589

Managing Editor: Tatiana Retivov

Book Design and Layout by Yulia Tymoshenko © 2019
Cover Design by Larisa Studinskaya © 2019
Original Photography by Gari Light © 2002-2020
Cover Photography by Anya Korolyova © 2014
Foreword by Tatiana Retivov © 2019

Published by
Bagriy & Company, Chicago, Illinois
www.bagriycompany.com

In Cooperation with
Kayala Publishing, Silver Spring, Maryland
www.kayalapublishing.com

Printed in the United States of America

CONTENTS

Additional Materials

FOREWORD

Gari Light could be described as a trilingual, contemporary American poet, based primarily in Chicago, yet his outlook and the subjects of his writings are truly interconnected and global. Gari originally hails from Kiev, having emigrated to America with his parents back in the late seventies, while in early adolescence. Even though his initial experiments with verse were in English, ironically he was more widely published in Russian. Some ten books in the span of the last thirty years, one of which is his English translation of Russian poet Aleksandr Kushner. Light also does not hide his childhood affinity to the Ukrainian language and hopes that some day there will be a collection of Ukrainian versions of his poetry published. Some of his poems have already been translated into Ukrainian by others.

In the last several years, however, Gari has been working on a book of poetry in English, as he has continued to write in that language all along. Some prose but mostly poetry, in rhyme and meter as well as in free verse, albeit sometimes a mixture of both can be found in the same poem. As the title of this book, "Confluences" vividly states, Light is well aware of how the puzzle comes to be whole: By staying open to the eclectic nuances of languages, cultures and emotions that comprise his poetry. In his more traditional verse Gari tends to ruminate upon the past and wax somewhat nostalgic. Echoes of Joseph Brodsky seep through his comparisons of rivers, lakes, seas, oceans, and other bodies of water (hence "Confluences") that can both divide and bring together nations and continents. Light also shares with Brodsky an intrinsic fondness for the harsh North.

The North persists in merciless winds and the rest and with its abusing, unbearable weather, / which only accentuates the outcome, being nonsensical and blurred as an indy feature should be

Light often casts urban entities as characters, while he makes his way through various European metropolises for work, or romantic sojourns, and reflects in detail upon each *mise-en-scène*. However, he never forgets where he came from, and the past often surfaces to haunt him as well as cause him to want to reckon with it:

First memory brought forth the Babiy Yar
from those ravines, I seek the answers even now
my phantom burns from bullet holes don't get me very far

It seems that Kiev, which his family left for good as they departed from the then Soviet Ukraine, is the proverbial organic and necessary must for this poet. His returns to the city are constant, both in verse as well as in person. Through the years he has become well known in Kiev literary circles for his poetry and songs, especially among bards who have put many of his Russian poems to music. It is as if he has never left, even though in reality for almost forty years his home has been elsewhere. Perhaps these are the realities of life in the 21-st century, that geographical exiles no longer exist as such. Light appears equally natural, at least in his writings, be it in the Bulgakov's "City" of his birth by the river Dnieper, or in what some call the most American of all American cities—Chicago, which is largely accentuated by the sea-like Lake Michigan; or in the Miami suburbs by the Atlantic Ocean, where his parents relocated from the Northern Midwest some years ago.

8

But one cannot write about Gari Light's poetry without mentioning the importance of Leonard Cohen, as it manifests itself in Light's poetic persona's state of prevailing melancholy interspersed with awe, lyrical though it may be. In fact, this entire collection can be said to have been written in homage to Cohen. One can see that he knows all of Leonard Cohen by heart, as he often seems to respond or send signals to his beloved teacher, in between strumming a guitar, lighting up a Gauloise, or observing a sunset. One of the most pronounced poems in "Confluences" describes the imaginary views from Leonard Cohen's window(s):

What Leonard Cohen saw from that hotel—on 23rd and 7th,
through the window
belongs to no one, yet to everyone, while contemplations still
remain within a choice...

It should also be noted that music and songwriting are important themes for the author of this book, and he frequently makes mention of a composer, musician, or songwriter in his poems, as well as quotes from songs. Yet, Gari Light can also be quite sardonic at times, especially when commenting on modern day mores of the dog-eat-dog business world. All romance goes out the window with this depiction of a contemporary networking session in Manhattan:

All welcome, our gratitude. Thank you for flying in,
as some of you did. Let's stay positive, shall we...
Yes, we realize that Aleppo is dying...
But first, let us pose for a cheerful group selfie.
And now: Let's discuss the role of art as notion—
wars end, there is always much joy in forgetting...

Although technically Light's poetry might seem to be more traditional than not, the overall tone and addressed issues are

9

quite contemporary and topical. Take, for example, his poem depicting the tragic *Battle of Ilovaisk* in Eastern Ukraine that took place in August of 2014, as Ukrainian Armed Forces and paramilitaries attempted to take back Ilovaisk, which had been captured by pro-Russian insurgents and Russian Armed Forces masquerading as paramilitaries. Despite the fact that Ukraine has been especially in the somewhat disastrous limelight lately, there is still so much hot air circulating between politicians who try to appear to be informed about the conflict. Where were these politicians in 2014? Sadly, this tragic battle of not such distant summer is going to go down in history as a classic example of modern day war, merciless and often senseless. Its relevance should not be underestimated. Because:

As lingering as that burning August air is the rhetorical question:
Who will be burdened with all the forgiving to be done...

Multingualism carries with it multiculturalism as well, it is the nature of the beast. In American poetry, it plays an especially important role, due to the nation's cultural melting pot. As a poet, Gari Light spans a couple of continents, countries, as well as eras, and bridges gaps through his poetry, in fact he loftily enters into a dialogue with his multicultural contemporaries, in the process of which the reader becomes acquainted with a new voice, a new world, specifically through the juxtaposition of different cultures. Such are the confluences contained in this poetry collection.

Tatiana Retivov,
Poet, translator, and
Director of Kayala Publishing
Kyiv, Ukraine
December 2019

To my Parents and Anya

A CONFLUENCE OF GRATITUDE

(An Author's Note of Sorts)

Come to think of it, there were no author's notes in any of my previously published books but one. Never really thought of reasons for that until now. Maybe that was because the previous ones were in another language, and certain norms that come with that do not make an author's note in a book a customary endeavor. Or maybe because I was a younger author then, and due to the combined arrogance, diffidence, inexperience and then some, thought that my mostly rhymed words contained in those books speak for themselves. As I noted in an author's comment in my relatively recent, and probably the most comprehensive collection, which was released simultaneously in Ukraine and in United States in 2017, by starting out and finishing off with a premise that there is really no need for an author's note, as "...what the author meant to project is still, most likely, best perceived from outside, even in such a subjective realm as poetry writing..."

And yet—here I go again. In retrospect, it is apparent, that at every stage of my life so far, I always lived close to a significant body of water. In the city of my childhood it was the great river. In the city of my adolescence and into the present, with some sequences of work-related absences—it is one of the great lakes. Lately, for large chunks of time of the last decade and counting—I find myself in the vicinity of one of the great oceans. It is not because confluences, as such are mostly water related, but precisely because symbolically they mean much more than that to me, is why I have chosen that word for this book's title.

Since childhood I was fascinated by the mostly abstract premise, that there are places on our planet, where smaller bodies of water enter, transform and become larger ones. I have always wanted to go to a place or two of this kind. The New York City area, where the East River, Hudson and the Atlantic do their thing, does not really count, as that place is miraculously surreal for a variety of other reasons.

As for poems contained in this collection: the majority of them were originally written in English, some of those appeared in the author's versions in my previous books published in Russian, both in the U.S. and abroad. A few of the poems here underwent the other kind of journey: Originally conceived in Russian, or less frequently in Ukrainian, they are being presented in English for the first time.

As a lawyer, mostly during the day—I am also obliged to remind the reader, and myself, while I am at it, that poetry writing is a very subjective realm. There is more often than not very little congruence (if any) between the author, and the narrator, when a poem is presented in the first person. As an author, perhaps I've lived through a few experiences reflected in the writings contained herein. However, poetic license, as opposed to the state or federal bar membership, does allow quite vast room for imagination. Some of the fabulas contained in the poetry here are what the author wished to have experienced, never did, yet tried to imagine the way in which they would have transpired. Others were imagined in a way not to wish upon anyone in reality. In any case, as it is all too common in legal disclaimers, but rare in poetry books: Any and all coincidences in these rhymed or unrhymed stanzas are purely incidental and do not refer to any particular individuals, times or events. Any and all resemblance to events, locales or persons, living or deceased are entirely coincidental. Just to be sure.

A few summers ago, my wife and I wound up in New Orleans, as guests at a wedding. The Mississippi river there looked especially eager to become one with the ocean, or at least with the Gulf of Mexico. I decided against looking up the area of that occurrence on line and elected to find out the old fashioned way—by asking the locals. Having been a big fan of Andrei Codrescu's poetry and radio commentaries for years, I figured that regulars at his favorite bar, Molly's, by the riverfront, should definitely know where the aforementioned metamorphosis occurs. My inquiry did not appear strange to a bunch of folks taking in the happy hour that summer afternoon. "You want to know where that particular confluence is," one of them asked, "that's not here, for sure, a bit further, a hundred miles or so, still in Louisiana though, I can get you approximate directions, but you better look it up on line, and best go during the day. Very easy to get lost in that area."

We never went to Plaquemines Parish that time, but the word "confluence", the way it was said and heard on that afternoon, certainly carried much symbolism in my recollection. By the time we left New Orleans, I pretty much decided that "confluence" would at least prominently figure in the title of my book of poetry in English. That is, of course, if I ever got brazen enough to make my English version poems public.

While edging closer to making this literary project a reality, I shared the possible title with a close friend in Chicago who is one of my musical co-authors on the album of songs made from my poems in Russian. The "Cohen Influence?!"—he asked, sounding somewhat bewildered, "right there in the title?" My friend is acutely aware, as many who know me are, of my special affinity with the literary heritage of Leonard Cohen. His poetry, for me, along with that of Boris Pasternak,

Federico Garcia Lorca, Elizabeth Bishop, Joseph Brodsky, Anna Akhmatova, W.H. Auden and Czeslaw Milosz, among numerous others, certainly serves as the beacon of inspiration. However, the poetry in this collection is wholeheartedly mine to answer for. When I finally understood that writing poems for me is not a passing phase, I almost wished for any and all influence of great poetic voices to be evident in what I do. However, whatever literary criticism actually noticed and reflected upon my earlier poetry collections, underscored my somewhat lonely path of not following in anybody's steps. The musical ear of my co-author, however, responding in the way that he did to the presence of the word "confluence" in the title inspired me. In fact, during the editing process, I noticed that of the few epigraphs that are present in the book—the overwhelming majority are from Leonard Cohen. Perhaps that is not a coincidence after all.

While the book was being prepared for publication and release, I was fortunate enough to share many of the texts that are featured in it during various literary events in the metropolitan Chicago and greater Miami areas. I owe much endless gratitude to the talented poets who heard me read, and offered their views on my work. Without those feedbacks, I probably would have continued to postpone this English version collection indefinitely. However, I knew that it was time to end any hesitation, when one of these great poets, while offering a most kind opinion as to my poetry, referred to the title of the book as "Confluences". In the plural, as there were quite a few by now. That's when everything finally came into place.

The poems in this collection contemplate, encompass and crisscross the cultures, languages, political, philosophical and geographical divides, and of course the beloved and grand bodies of water. One of the numerous confluences connected with this book is also an unintended coincidence, that it is

15

being released almost precisely to the day when forty years ago my early adolescence ended in the old world and began in the new one. For that I owe a tremendous debt of gratitude to my parents, who as first generation immigrants persevered and succeeded in this most amazing country in the world. In the process, they also somehow managed to insure that the values, which were dear to them, reflected and continued in their son. I deem this to be my biggest accomplishment. In dedicating this book to my parents—Gina and Boris, as well as to my wife Anya, is just a drop into the confluence of love and gratitude that I am fortunate to experience.

Gari Light
Evanston, Illinois
December, 2019

IF ONE'S FATED TO BE BORN IN CAESAR'S EMPIRE,
LET HIM LIVE ALOOF, PROVINCIAL, BY THE SEASHORE...
—JOSEPH BRODSKY

ALL IS SILVER: THE HEAVY SURFACE OF THE SEA,
SWELLING SLOWLY AS IF CONSIDERING SPILLING OVER...
—ELIZABETH BISHOP

I AM UNDERWATER AND MY HEARTBEATS MAKE
CIRCLES ON THE SURFACE...
—MILAN KUNDERA

I

"We Haven't Walked Those Sands"

We haven't walked those sands sufficiently enough,
haven't quite felt the essence of the desert deep down inside.
The front line artillery rounds were loaded with blanks.
Our worst fears—merely resulting in partially grey temples.
The reassessment—did not appear to be among the good omens
The truly good and kind were no longer the preferred choice,
just as that old feeling of empathy wasn't missed when It vanished
into the morning dawn ocean, leaving no reflections at all.
That awkward listing of apparent triumphs was so lonely and rash
that the resulting moral lapses would not be absolved with tears in time.
The countdown had begun: It was pathetic, sad and quiet.
The breeze touched the bedroom curtains in the midst...
It would be unbecoming to share any further details.
And all while that fairytale was set in biblical proportions,
the Pharisaism went unheeded, but for the perception of light.
Darkness managed to hide itself quite well in distant corners,
hinting of its impending arrival in periodic ghoulish outbursts.
Arrived, it did, November evening, in the feeble count of votes,
and was distributed so loudly that some have chosen not to hear at all.
That time, which is adjusting still... The fort abandoned, not yet taken,
the books of longing and forgiving, have not been ordered yet to burn...
As the draft decree is still lacking that coma, not that grammar matters,
and when it all becomes a roar, when all indulgences have been granted,
it will be a free for all, a transparent festival of hatred.
The pain caused would linger, as the pendulum had swung,
It may be quite late, as the edge of hope becomes visible,
and while the choice remains as given, there are apparently—
no takers anymore

* * *

The odds are there to beat...

—Leonard Cohen

A brighter ray of sharp perceptions comes to life—
comes from within, it's pondering and subtle
such imperfection of the clouds feeds all strife,
subconscious childhood resurfaces to stutter...
The year before Prague witnessed Russian tanks,
apparent spring succumbed to winter's echo,
our parents braved the cold (so many thanks!).
And we appeared to fill the void of murdered brethren...
First memory brought forth the Babiy Yar
from those ravines, I seek the answers even now
my phantom burns from bullet holes don't get me very far,
the pain excruciating, as I bow...
Our genetic burden overall,
is of the sort one wouldn't wish as wind on willows,
don't even notice petty theft at all,
as our thoughts are on the march to Salaspils.
Not much has changed, equator measures still,
yet a brighter ray will always pierce the cloud cover
Who had forgiven, perpetrators, victims will...
Deadlock in rhetoric—there's nothing to discover.
Yet we appeared—the odds were there to beat,
our core peculiar, on verge of constant tearing
We won't give up the corner of our street,
Despite attempts of present Goebbels, Hess or Goering

Let the Ocean Behold

Let the ocean behold
the reflection of the heavens,
then—refute the misconceptions
of it being soft and tender
with Cesaria Evora
or the sounds of *brasiliero*,
be absolved now and forever,
of attempts on soul collecting,
as it's wedged into horizons
as an optical illusion
of all those who gazed and wandered
through the waters, being mortal...
It is not a panacea,
nor is it a cleansing being,
but it rather Is an owner
of all those repeated errors
by those self-absorbed fanatics
who were always so certain
at the end appearing blind...
Let the ocean behold
the mundane understanding of nature,
on the hope that it isn't vindictive

Leonard Cohen's View from the Window

Those were the reasons and that was New York...
—Leonard Cohen

What Leonard Cohen had seen of the outside—an island view
not Hydra, yet sufficing...
For those impressions, which curtail sadness:
fire escapes, their complex intertwining,
across the street—there was a laundromat
as well as a delightful Cantonese joint,
a little awkward, yet delicious and fulfilling...
He also saw an entrance to a shrine, yet not the store,
full of guitars and other gear...
as Janice blocked the view while she wished for
another kind of joy, completely different,
All the while it appeared to her that she descended,
and not the other way around...
Over her shoulder, just beyond the window,
he contemplated such arrays of magic
which rarely appear when in confluence
even with such discreet circumstances,
they can't be sung, or written down, just that moment...
Yet Leonard Cohen from his window saw it all:
Manhattan sky of such amazing kind,
that later on he wouldn't comprehend it,
he also wouldn't know how the hell
the buildings and the sirens simply vanished...
All indications were—the world as such,
apparently was ending, yet,
the weather folks provided explanations
less drastic for New Yorkers to consider...
Then he remembered his beloved Montreal,
where certain happenings were also quite frequent,

especially in those interpretations that were Suzanne's,
as when she goes down...
Abruptly to the river, in November,
it's cold and windy, in accordance to the text...
What Leonard Cohen saw from that hotel—
on 23rd and 7th, through the window
belongs to no one, yet to everyone, while contemplations
still remain within a choice...
What Leonard Cohen saw appeared spellbound,
quite impossible in diametric vision:
Burnt by the sun, the future of Key West,
where he is being tried in Russian versions,
Ironically, the best attempt belongs to an enigma of the past
so full of doubts
as to her talent and her beauty even more. Her role had ended.
Yet, coming of off her protracted absence,
she suddenly appeared some years later in a brief encounter,
by very random chance,
on an intersection of that island, which belonged
to Leonard Cohen's view from "Chelsea" in the 60's...
Back then, he somehow managed to foresee
the future in the way of certain sketches
made out of music, sounds and some words
which are enlightened by the volume of his kind.
They balance out those under the moon
which contradict the harmony of light...
And therefore, that window at the "Chelsea"
forever will belong to Leonard Cohen,
Who saw it all, that night of love with Janice ..
His wisdom's for the morrow, not today

Zoned

There is rain in the comfort zone
and a crawling fog.
The sky is uneasy, there's
promise of things to come.
The time of the year
possesses a certain flow,
the overwhelming demand being
a topless muse and exquisite bourbon.

It has been a while since
there were tall ships in port,
runways are no longer
used at the airfield,
the stubborn ones await
a certain event of sorts:
They searched and purged
his abode of medicine.

Then there is she sleeping
alone at night, the one getting
interrogated during the day.
Afterwards she returns to her flat,
takes a long shower, lacking repentance.
There are no shades on the window,
As well as no meanings as such,
a machine gun is set at the theater stage.
Such a blunt yet symbolic move
affects the song, a good looking death
reflects in the windows with glimmering lights

a flock of ravens unable to fly is on hold.
Fortune tellers and tarot card readers
recently burned at the barn *en masse*,
That calmed the crowds, as order was briefly restored.
A bunch of surgeons took care
of the grass at the stadium field,
and a certain shadow hangs
over the main façade.
Meanwhile both he and she
have made the list
for particular trains bound east,
her guitar in the theater dressing room,
a draft of his novel as well.
Yet both come short of delivering grace.
Of course, in retrospect,
this particular segment of time
would come to be known as medieval.
A time when horseshoes cease
all effort of leaving marks,
and those who remain,
will even attempt to return.
Yet for now
the forecast calls
for some fog and rain,
the comfort zone is
legislatively set to be gone.
The essence being not
in the time of year,
but simply in the time
that has come to regret
such a petty and sad outcome

"Not Autumn Yet"

Not autumn yet—will say the Harlequin,
the eternal second in del arte hierarchy,
as autumn is accompanied by sadness,
and other motives deemed to be pathetic...
"Such nonsense bores me," Joaquin chimes in,
who burned himself within the throes of ardor
"America is lacking nowadays
time of the year really notwithstanding."
"You, gentlemen, are beasts," so whispers Olga,
whose image has been snatched by demon chaser
"the horrors you will witness in the future,
your winters will be hot, the summers freezing."
"I don't belong!" bewildered mutters Wolfgang,
effected by such tone and odd demeanor,
"Your burning shackles hardly set in timing,
you are naïve, and bordering on reckless..."
"You all are wrong," opined de la Fère,
By masking issues. Such rhetoric and glamour,
while giving in both the philosophy and splendor...
Love is at fault. The one, that's spiced by passion.
Then Agaspher, perpetually tired, he's seen it all in time
will reconcile, all who have spoken and those who haven't:
The essence is to find a way home, to get there,
that's the ultimate of "Happy"

* * *

Occasions with no breaking news on screens,
where there is only silence, foliage and autumn,
the coveted departure from all deeds
from city streets to forests at the bottom
of mountains... She takes her makeup off,
pristine and beautiful, yet so full of magic
matter-of-fact and trivially tender
her glance subliminal, yet fleeting and nostalgic.
It makes you stay and cancel rides and flights,
breathe in the dawn, no words are really needed,
forsaking parting for a myriad of nights,
with all the heaven's promises unheeded.
All such temptations solemnly defied
with disbelief and posturing abandoned,
the truth and her appearance coincide
with a year's end in all the lights and splendor

Retroesque

When they say—repent, repent—
I wonder what they meant...
—Leonard Cohen

Fast becoming old-fashioned, or be it as it may:
—I was always that way, admittedly.
Not reacting, withholding acceptance, and frequently late.
The barricades, the quintessence of pain—
resulting in injuries and smoke...
Astonished by the heroism, except that...
Death is real, more often than not.
Much delight in the progress of science,
which casually, as a matter of fact
had surpassed science fiction's most forward looking
predictions of the 60's and 70's,
but what they had not come up with yet, had they...
Is what's to be done, when suddenly
a heart stops... Not many innovations in that field on record yet.
In our future, the one that is here and now today,
Unrequited love still remains what it is,
an anomaly, frequent and dull,
no remedy still as to what to do with the glances,
and the blades of pronounced words,
which leave those horrific cuts
that do not become scars for long in all of the souls involved.
What really is strange though
is that the stars are still so far out of reach,
that their occasional tumbling downs are hardly enough
to grant all the wishes simultaneously wished for,
there is only that childhood memory of the old fishing boat,
gliding over the moonlit river
where the miracle hides in the mere semi-circle move of the paddle,
in that passing second.

I am not masking that retroesque essence of mine,
certainly not repenting, merely admitting to it.
It must be so painful becoming amber still,
but it is apparently the touch of impeccable beauty,
As childhood reminiscences continue to lure
toward the sweet fleeting sadness,
where there were no apparent losses,
while that imagined bliss was being written in cursive

Contemplating Victoria Island

To wake up in the Canadian wilderness,
by the sea, of course, in the provinces,
getting there the night before on an old ferry
from a half-forgotten seaport in the States...
The preferences here are—pencils instead
of key strokes, not latte, just coffee. Plain,
The floorboards creak in the old house,
and there is an omnipresent fog in all windows.

Staring at the horizon, forgetting all that's unnecessary,
just pondering on rhymes and meter
tailoring the words properly, prior to placing them in stanzas...
Burning the tongue with that coffee,
getting up and walking in the sea mist,
realizing that it is pouring rain, where umbrella is sudden.
Gathering a handful of synonyms
whispering lines in the process, on the way to the local marina.

Then taking on something different: what it would really be like,
how would it all turn out,
if the staffer for that global non-profit, in Rome,
in the first year of the now far away iconic 80s
Would say—why go to America?—
summers are brutally scorching over there...
Let's think of Canada, it's kinder and more sentimental—
that's where we would have you land.

That proverbial solitaire naturally ended up
with a slightly different, predictable outcome,
there were some riddles remaining,
perhaps in the language nuances of accents and dialects...
Yet, the overall tasks and milestones
were being resolved in a quite responsible manner,

the skeptics, surely, in their favorite mode
would point to some residue of minor decadence.

And nevertheless, periodically, while waiting at ferry crossings,
there are perspectives to muse,
Not so much from the lingering fact
that the transitory truth is semi-tonal and partly transparent,
that's when those who deem themselves to be stoic prophets,
knowing it all, will morally fail.
While dogmatic beads scatter,
and what appeared naive and banal becomes inherently evil.

And now with the fairway being passed,
in the midst of the journey, the preferences transform:
There is the profound need to sojourn in the provinces,
foggy and rainy islands being the choice,
and on the way back, as seen from miles up,
within the sound of jet engines,
preferring the opposite of the post-modernist theatrical mutterings,
and choosing *The Seagull*

Accepting the gift in the order of words
that somehow are put together on your initiative,
You glance at the mountain edges
from the fishing pier salted and aged by years of yearning,
you have forgotten the names of those,
formerly unimagined of being without, but managed,
and even the previously absurd scenarios of reality
gain all sorts of meanings and make sense.

At the time when vanishing visions disappear
into an announcement of the boarding process,
and a remnant of a somewhat alert perception
slides off to the side, and suddenly vanishes,
as the contour of the sky results
in a quiet and astonishing epiphany,
followed by that sound made at conception,
bestows the resulting miracle humbly and somewhat equally

"The Sound Comes Along"

The sound comes along because
the silence is akin to chalk that crumbles,
a guitar chord so hesitant and random
echoes in the fading remnants of departing steps.
There's a sudden appearance of notes and contours,
as if being dictated, with no need for drafts,
in that unison of music and verse,
where Sabbath rolls in the veil of a different fate
along with the fog taking over the city,
covering the Landscape alley[1], daring the odds...
As if nurturing those who crossed the ocean
to where it all began, with a gentle guitar.
Nevertheless, it means so much,
when both of the River's banks
are so vividly tangible and visible,
as if the miracles took place
with the tears of the ones you love
turning into the reflection of the dew.
It shines on Monastery[2] domes, becoming light,
In Paradzhanov's cinematic answers...
It is that summer, the last one before the war,
when in the sky over the domes there is a sign...
The sound comes along because
the silence sets ahead of sadness
the sunset so far beyond
recalls that unison of music and verse

---

[1] An artistic throughfare in Kyiv, Ukraine.

[2] An Orthodox Vydubetsky Monastery in Kyiv, Ukraine.

* * *

Who is a person in a cat's realm?
Lord only knows, as does the cat herself a little...
She met us at the threshold of our home
not caring much what century it was.
When so nonchalantly, free of charge
she cleared the mind's surface of all worries,
her glance throughout being so light and warm...
On the subconscious level her love
was so inexplicable, so true and selfless
even the trees of that November from outside
gestured so kindly to her through foggy windows.
She really asked for nothing in return,
reading our minds and sending us good omens...
She had no clue how we would cry non-stop
when she abruptly died that cold Thanksgiving.
That slice of our existence ended sharply,
her being gone is not some awful nightmare...
What is a cat in the human universe is still
not much defined by experience and reason...
It's just—we miss her so very much

A New England Tale

It's the nineties recalled—
coffee, cigarettes, destiny doubts,
in the handful of days as a break
in pursuit of the present,
when the winter is ready to exit,
there suddenly comes a realm to consider:
simple essence—an evening,
a flight, slightly turbulent landing.
95th Interstate in that state,
which is buried in snow and almost forgotten...
On the right, sudden exit to that adolescent endeavor,
which had ended abruptly,
in a certain amalgam of trembling air,
where New York is assumed to be near,
and a memory comes of those sad
collect-call conversations on Saturday evenings
when a father and son have so little to say,
while battling tears in being apart.
Then New England became a harmonious prelude
to that other England in Britain
and the two came together in just a few years,
which seemed to be consciously longer...
As a fallen guitar, which was dropped from the bed,
as she sighed out loud,
and she did so piercingly, knowing that circumstances are such,
that this marriage is over...
In that England there were no continued,
safe premonitions of Paris,
even though they were there in the depth

of the several hours under the Channel
"I would never forget you..."[1]
but won't insult you with mercy,
if I ever by accident see you,
it just happens that way—we become inexorably older...
Once in palindrome autumn,
again wound up in New England with a dream of a woman,
It was so insane, that the crowd around decided it wasn't to be,
with a staged opposition
we just sat in the car, taking in the surroundings,
hurting each other with silence—
it was mute, while pain upon swallowing,
simply established the loss, as it happened...
When it snows in New England, It does so for real,
and literal walls of the snow abound,
I'm suddenly feeling provincial,
the one who is not scared of whiteouts, a child of snow—
when that blizzard was crushing the roofs as if drunk and abandoned,
I recall something else—that monster snow in '77,
It reflected in memory over the ocean...
Those were the dear European beginnings in Kiev

---

[1] A line from Andrei Voznesensky's poem from the rock opera libretto *Junos and Avos*.

* * *

Werther is already written, the sail is white,
it all would work out on other occasions.
That crack in the name—time is certainly trite,
If even the setting is slightly voracious.
Those childhood dreams with the sea in reflections,
caressing the dock, which had ceased to be coastal,
the meanings no longer debated in sessions
Liszt's rhapsodies are irreversible, mostly.
The wish is to know with certain abandon,
that words are, in fact, being candidly honest,
but Werther is written, the white sail is stranded,
she is playing the piano, just like it was promised.
Her hands in the fog do appear to be ghostly
as if they were never raised up to the heavens,
the musical sounds end up being costly,
they float through the windows, clock dies at eleven.
Abandonment sounds as hopeless as winter,
where neither a sigh nor a step would be real,
confluence of faith at the hands of the minter...
Werther is written, the white sail is here

Jerusalem

Jerusalem has gone to rest,
and left the doors unlocked.

It is a city of winters, which are rare and magical,
where blizzards cannot be predicted.

It is a hearth of unquenchable passions,
that fell so low, and were raised so high,

It is a land of laughing and crying children,
and imported cherries, which are delivered unripe.

This is the place of Calvary and eternal walls,
of hopes, ideas, definitions and revelations.

What would it be without Helens,
without temples of various faiths and all-night vigils...

The greatness of it tends to upbraid,
the ancient ever-present mysticism of it humbles.

Beyond the realm of the Procurator's dilemma,
be it, before, after, presently or in the future,
one may only be in awe of these walls and the sky

August. Morning. The Current War

The Army captain was dying
in a vivid sunflower field in Ukraine.
From that morning there remained
just a third of the battery charge in his phone,
and some lingering minutes of credit.
It was clear to the captain:
There will be no mercy to anyone captured,
as there would be no welcoming music,
to whoever escaped this calamity whole and alive,
as the price of a life was declining abruptly.
All night long, after a bloody and desperate day,
he led a diminishing platoon of young soldiers-survivors
through the fields and ravines under heavy artillery rounds
as the Russians,
abundant in their ammunition reserves kept it coming,
distributing death in measured proportions...
It appeared that the air was burning
as were all the sharpened remnants of the officer's oath...
In the morning, a Russian sharpshooter picked out
the rest of the most inexperienced fighters
from the captain's platoon,
while wounding the captain, denying him use of his legs,
which he covered in soil.
As the captain observed, the enemy was closing in,
getting out through shallow ravines was no longer an option.
He took out his old but reliable phone
and attempted to dial a number in Kyiv,
at home, on the left bank of the Dnieper,
his wife answered in jubilant voice:

Dear, finally! We were so worried,
the nightmares we see are so awful,
you really should try and call more often,
you are exhausting us with all these worries,,,
As his daughter, a student accepted to study abroad,
then grabbed the phone and demanded:
come home soon daddy, we really miss you...
He envisioned them both in the kitchen,
watching American sitcoms on the Soviet era TV,
while the captain—in and out of consciousness, smiled and spoke:
Girls, I love you so much!
What's with those pesky felines of ours—the carpet destroyers?
How are things with "Dinamo",
good soccer, are they on the ball,
as the season is rolling?...
A battered, bullet-ridden Ukrainian army emergency ambulance
somehow got through the encirclement,
and suddenly appeared from nowhere,
as the nurse and the doctor tried to get the captain inside...
The Russian tanks were fast approaching from the side of the ravine...
The ringing...It was either a church bell or a concussion...
The captain could not really tell.
The paratroopers who followed the tanks shot the nurse dead right away..
They were hesitating as to what to do with the doctor,
when one of the Russian officers appeared to have recognized him—
they were in the same Soviet unit serving in Afghanistan in the 80's...
Thus, August of 2014 burned over Ukraine... The captain was dying.
It shall forever remain unclear whether
there was reproach in the eyes of the captain.
As lingering as that burning August air is the rhetorical question:
Who will be burdened with all the forgiving to be done...
In accordance with the unspoken terms of the criminal elite, or conceivably
through the guidance of the Scriptures or perhaps the concepts
                                        of the Qur'an?..

One Day in Winter, Spring and Summer...

The other day in winter, spring and summer,
saperlipopette of stopovers feeds the drama
and then again the amplitude that varies,
Neruda quotes, which make you think of Paris.
Searching for words, when stuck in fluctuation
at times, when you are met with jubilation,
more often though, it is the other way around
emotions of the negative abound...
Take-off is swift, the pilots' skills are awesome
"beyond the flesh, the beauty is colossal"
Air corridor becomes Missouri-Kansas,
the storms and turbulence are echoing in stanzas,
is a pattern to the South really worth the trouble,
perhaps the learning curve will count for double.
Not much of anything that will be so written,
blog comments will be sinister and bitter.
Yet, what as a result will not transpire,
provides the niche to this particular esquire.
The soundtrack of the beloved "Rigoletto",
assures smooth landing in Miami, which is better,
than the beginning of this journey in Chicago...
And did Neruda really miss Santiago?..

Leap Year Sublime

Those rains in the ocean appeal to me more than the snows of Lake Michigan,
as they happen in February, leap year being the setting,
when the edge of horizon does appear to be lacking corrosion,
I'm confessing to being tranquil and impressed by its seeming perfection.
The sun glare that is trying so hard to be fictional rather than real
is taking the path of the early attempts at poetry by Mayakovsky—
at this point the demagogy already endured by the planet is astonishing,
and that is merely to prove that it is, indeed, anything but flat.
All the attempts undertaken negating the coast in appearing subliminal
are almost convincing, surprisingly sounding truthful,
when, in that phantom ovation dissolving in running waves,
playing with leaves, which are so discreet and unusual...
Yes, all is relative when the warmth is a substance of value and interest,
when by the lake, all we get are the remnants and memories...
Rare is a February every four years and counting, so mysterious
it's the guitar which gives rise to the lyrical poetry,
that inspiration is restless in sharing wholeheartedly,
which it undercuts with the ideas of Sextus Empiricus...
And so be it with rains in the ocean and lake effect snowstorms—
they are essential in wishing and making a melody,
and when confirming the notion in prose or in poetry,
which are dictated from the above with a whisper and honesty

An Epiphany

Let's just get there again —
to that unforgettable place,
where the rain, as it falls
whispers names on the cobblestone surface,
let's just get there whenever,
be it spring as the lilacs make it insane,
or the fall, when the leaves as they perish,
do it through all the magic of seeing...
Let's just get there again,
just to marvel and witness
all those images
that are impossible to be described.
Let's not bring anything,
let those matters remain somewhere else—
all the pain and forebodings,
betrayals and merciless doubts
will be all written off
as superfluous things of the past...
As we are taken in by this island of hope,
in the midst of the city.
As we walk, we'll encounter those
transient remnants of childhood dreams,
which may not be interpreted,
logically followed, or witnessed and conquered.
We would suddenly, out of nowhere —
wholeheartedly start to believe,
in the way which some cynics
will never succeed in convincing
us to reconsider.

Will just wonder here all afternoon,
as the twilight takes over the river,
as the synagogues, churches and mosques,
cast reflections of light
through the shadows,
permeating epiphany,
simple and true as the air,
and the words that
are better unspoken...
Let's just get there again,
to enable that flow of events,
which were always foretold,
but so rarely happen in times,
when the miracles are ridiculed
by the soulless and clever,
yet, those latter will lose,
just as long as we get there on time.
Let's just get there again

Manhattan. Early Spring'16.
Networking. Monologue

All welcome, our gratitude. Thank you for flying in,
as some of you did. Let's stay positive, shall we...
Yes, we realize that Aleppo is dying...
But first, let us pose for a cheerful group selfie.
And now: Let's discuss the role of art as notion—
wars end, there is always much joy in forgetting...
(...that's where someone causes an unneeded commotion,
by mentioning Eastern Ukraine and bloodletting...)
The speech was renewed in a monologue format:
We came to the States as its saving messiahs,
yet, some of us dwell in the liberal orbit,
but those are so few—Russophobes and pariahs...
Again, we digress—and as beautiful people,
let's plan on Bolshoy coming here in the winter...
That guy from the Midwest—cut it out with that snicker,
your presence is really becoming a splinter...
We heard of your lawyerly deeds for illegals,
who laughably claim prosecution in Russia.
What's next? Equal rights for those fickle vegans?
Trump wins in November and stops these discussions...
Where were we? All right, our friends from Gosduma[1]
are willing to come, speak to us in the summer,
right after UN, where they're fighting the tumor
of those who are trying to bring Putin down...
Hey you, from Chicago, your laugh is annoying
stop being disturbing, we're watching in mirrors
we thumbed through your books of so-called poems,
and spat on such words for five hundred years

---

[1] The lower house of parliament of the Russian Federation.

* * *

When ease of comfort unexpectedly descends
to cups of tea, having abandoned walls and ceiling,
and evening lilac dispenses fragrant favors
when sudden sadness finds refuge in Chopin,
not randomly Chopin—his interjections...
To be particular, as one should try in May,
is it the dusk or twilight which become
coincidences—silent, yet so bright,
it's the occurrence of non-rhyming lines.
Such a catharsis notwithstanding answers,
and subtle words without the slightest chance
during the time of drizzle and the wind,
when spring was shy and slightly trembling...
Then comes the evening in mid-May,
from inconspicuous collisions fate defined,
stating so graciously and softly—this is love

II

Cinematique

.

Disparity of time, as if accused of being faithful,
horizon pales with light, exhaling dusk, unfitting...
...So inappropriate, bewildering. The glow
is subsequential to what shines through the window.
Across the empty plaza walks a dog, a stray,
no claims to anything, but hunger...
It's raining. Not a hint of the deluge,
more than a drizzle though the mood settles on romantic
as both of them emerge from the hotel in Prague
or Venice. For the script, it's not important.
A close-up to the bed, it's empty now,
then to the curtains which are swaying gently,
as if not from the breeze but from the abandoned
motion of love, or rather—that emotion, left vague
and not developed for the film...
They're walking to the crossing, hand in hand.
Of course, she is dark haired. He is smoking
a cigarette... It borders on cliché, but the co-production
of this film has made allowances for the tired melancholy.
No intimacy, though. There were takes. Her olive skin
reflected quite subtly against his not so exemplary physique.
Those shots were cut in favor of the walk, which is symbolic
in the way he holds her hand... She smiles...
...A panorama of the crossing in Berlin, Donetsk or Sarajevo...
The script is not particular on that. They walk on the wet
cobblestones to separate carriages, parting without saying a word...
Credits roll to Stravinsky's "Enchanted Garden"

Thirty-Five Miles Above

All indicators confirm the fact that Paris is gone,
those early flights have quite a lot in common,
the airline coffee appears to be real only to some,
and literary nuances are just like the verbs that summon.
The struggling moon is dissolved in the zodiac sign,
the month just began and winter is approaching fast,
while all it should take is to be understanding and kind,
as that fugue composed by Bach is a sensory test.
They both added a year within a margin of error,
the ensuing century, such a minuscule mark nowadays—
Inherently beautiful, yet she is probably frozen with terror,
when the lines of Garcia Lorca appear in past tense.
This subject matter, while thirty-five miles above the ocean,
is sort of nuanced in "what would happen" and "when"...
He is sipping the duty-free whiskey, resisting the notion
to drop her a line, actually doesn't, and counts to ten...
Then the Hudson valley appears in the round window,
confirming for good, that Paris is certainly far away—
yet the poetry lines, so written, were not rescinded—
no edits needed, those stanzas were sort of a dream anyway

A Solo for the Morning Snow

And sometimes when the night is slow...
You lose your grip and then you slip
Into the masterpiece...
   —Leonard Cohen

All efforts to create in real time
a masterpiece would definitely fail,
as inspiration does not get to become
incarnate from Neverland,
yet there may be a single instance,
where such a premise may cast a doubt—
and that is when the last exclamation
of December floats by your window.

A woman wakes—the mascara
on her eyelashes remaining from last night,
marking a semicircle of fate...
The reflection of unearthly crystal flows,
would sparkle in the vain desires of eternity,
when evenings miraculously gray
attempted to set the rules of the game.

Yet, all is otherwise in this sudden snowstorm,
All along, the glance embraces a confluence
of the water's edge with the sky,
as the white exquisite flakes appear
only to turn into celestial numbers...
The awakened woman wears nothing,
and such heavenly garb is subtly befitting,
as her victory is merely a reflection of defeat,
as if in the case of the fallen snow
and its reincarnation not really fitting into words

Modigliani's Leap February

Leap February arrives as a sign of grievances past—
in the sharpness of collisions.
The fireplace still lingers, while dusk turns into twilight
in anticipation of the dark, as they...
Appear to be stumbling in the pronunciation
of rarely spoken Italian words and sentences,
water is everywhere, there are unexplained splashes in the canals,
as the shadows dissipate.

Here it goes again—this last winter's month is leap indeed,
its arrogance on full display,
yet silk abounds in it as well,
along with the guitar chords rolling beyond the sands of the Lido.
Outside the windows the carnival is unwrapping
as if a high category hurricane in its full glory,
it is as tempting as the night reflected
in the masked beauty that brought the invite to the ball.

There is such a numbing temptation to respond
to her invitation with a mere nod, the moon
being her vivid accomplice with cat-like moves,
there is no say what the consequences will bring
when she takes all of her promises back
with a nonchalant half smile while at *Ponte dei Sospiri*,
Nevertheless, he would always...
There will never be a day, when his door is locked for her.

Water reflections contain images of so many exotic flowers,
that the colors appear unearthly.

Venice is reluctantly preparing to welcome
the first edges of dawn along the echoing steps,
The month of February is so blazingly awkward
in having that tricky extra day, and yet...
All of his sketches are of her in various states of undress,
and all her poems are still about him.
No need for all of those useless torturous borders,
continents and mile distances between them.
That initial benevolent flaw in their love,
is not even attempted to be veiled by those two,
especially in this decadent month,
whose plight is to be always divisible by four,
except once in four. On the day, which has no place or purpose,
but one of burning evidence in the fireplace.

It is in early March, when their shared
delusional detours finally come to an obvious end.
Back to Montmartre from the doomed city of water,
magical decay and bridges of tears and sighs
Spring usually arrives with a few tasks,
among them the necessity of sewing up the hearts,
and assuring dignified and formal sweep of the fallout
for all of those affected by the leap month

A Reflection of Palindrome August

Then that August was coming tomorrow.
No changes were needed, and things were all right,—
it was sort of foretold,
in that act of the autumn's conception in faraway lands...
She got lucky with parking in Lincoln Park West,
came upstairs, and got on an ominous flight,
of the kind that needs to take off, then establish the pattern,
and never apparently ends.
All that calendar nonsense was strangely amusing,
and then on occasion was solemnly odd—
when it snowed in May, or when January rain
cried through foreplay of simmering spring.
Just that way she pronounced in Russian
the name of the last summer month,
while being completely exhausted
by the constantly challenging order of things...
It's futile—putting things in perspective that palindrome year,
but not even once
was there even a hint
that it would last undeniably through that summer and fall.
Or that the future may take them to Venice, the Moon,
or at least to the roads of Provence,
they were both so tired of previous doubts,
and errors of judgement were certainly taking their toll.
August came many times since the one
that they actually managed to sail across,
and come every October, with so many years
being gone to the side of the imminent past,
when they suddenly meet in the realm
of infrequent yet warm and elaborate dreams...
No one claims any drama,
or what could have been—
if it was to last...
Just as August becoming September,
in French or Italian films, never is what it seems

Hearing Rain in September

Have you ever seen the rain?[1]
—John Fogerty

How long has it been since you heard the rain?
You are aware that particularly in September
the rain veils neither sorrow, nor the fragrance of the sky.
It does rustle the leaves in the doomed foliage though,
striving so hard not to appear prophetic,
while being an unwitting forerunner of the snow.

That night rain in September
had this certain rhetorically tart clarity,
like the wine, which is not in the bottles, just yet...
Fermentation still being a process,
so most likely they're still Napa grapes in those valleys,
than a favorite drink of the idle.

You are probably hearing through sleep,
such a tender and quivering whisper which is sketching
the autumn so gently inside destinies, horoscopes, notebooks
When you wake in the morning, believe it—
doubts serve no particular purpose...
You'll be much better off trusting the whispers
of that rain in September... By far

---

[1] "Have You Ever Seen the Rain" is a song written by John Fogerty and released as a single in 1971 from the album Pendulum (1970) by rock group Creedence Clearwater Revival.

That Evening in the Fall

As Pushkin said:
the time when eyes are charmed
dispenses favors so cautiously and gently,
it's almost reckless,
and so inherently it slows and beholds,
as if bewildered, stopping for a while,
and then proceeds towards this phase
of miracles and tenderness in autumn,
so unpredictable and even borderline.
A trembling leaf announces farewell
to the remaining—very last of butterflies,
whose image, as celestially seen—
reflects in Scorpio, which is a stubborn woman
so tired of appearing to be fragile,
and yet she does appear so
while veiled in dancing solo.

It is that seasonal forgiving
that streamlines the blessings
and the novelty of love...
Or so it seemed during the springtime of emotions
while settling through the summer into this
untouchable prelude, with songs and teasing...
Becomes foreseeable and even sort of magic—
a sky that lately lingered quite low
instead of rain dispenses snowy lace and covers all,
not following the rules, creating routes,
so carelessly imagined in flowing dreams

which vanish in the slow morning dusk,
defining as useless subtle movements
that for a bit controlled the narrative as such.
The glance discovers refuge in horizon,
and then it gradually, slowly disappears
while discovering—it is, of course the lake,
and not the ocean for a change,
that is imperative to knowing—indeed,
what Pushkin said so long ago, rules eternal

* * *

When snow is fresh and wet... Four days after New Year's.
A new century was born—the weather brave on pillows.
As I recall, Lake Michigan was cast as the Solaris
the way it breathed, its color and walks along were brisk and wise.
In Tarkovsky's original—they parted both in life and thereafter.
Nonetheless, that winter, so fidgety—no one drastically suffered...
In a truly midsummer December that preceded the lyrical narrative,
in retrospect, it seems to be the color of amber, its end comparative.
Not necessarily destined for horseshoes on the Lincoln Park pavement,
nor the wishes unspoken but warm, or for the candle light to remain.
Such is January's fate—the beginning, as opposed to the harrowing sequels
of snowy birthdays, as if in the seventh inning—becoming strangely
                                                    familiar equals

Revelation in Little Havana

Little Havana fool moon—
treacherous tango—the first of May,
the whole thing is so much on the edge,
of course neither the guitar nor tea transpired,
Likewise, in Paris a while back
neither jazz nor coffee at *Saint-Germain-des-Prés*,
No bargains at the book stalls on the left bank of the Seine,
no Czech artist's pencil song,
No chianti ever by the Lagoon,
no "sesterces from a flesh that covers",
No runes on fire by San Marco Square,
just because the hell with it all...
That old Barcelona pier,
where on the telephone "once upon an autumn"
the dialogue appeared to be ghostly,
as if being supernatural, and serving as a mere reflection...
No encounters whatsoever in Moscow,
at any of the magical sights noted by Bulgakov,
the yellow flowers did turn out to be leaves
in Chicago's Lincoln Park, much later though...
No Kiev, be it a subjunctive or otherwise
In Little Havana, a weightless moonlight
streamed itself through the tree shadows, for no reason

Pathetic Random Musings
on the Muse

A pity we don't get to choose our muse,
the muse herself is not particularly eager
to incarnate as if her own antidote,
no union of muses would defend her right as such.
Not all of them, (the muses), but a few
to gain our departure from the script
would even ponder thoughtful disrobing,
but once our palm gains access to the place,
where a muse's heart is usually located,
a muse arrives at the painful conclusion:
That going forward, we don't really care
how lonely she may get in being worshipped,
as in the process we become annoying
not only to the muse, but to ourselves
and honestly, to everybody else...
As we cut through the muse's libido
her essence, also, while being at it,
we would neglect to offer anesthesia,
while removing the muse's wings,
as they don't fit the rhyme or meter even,
and yet we so passionately lie to Casper,
or to another friendly ghost,
that we would never dare give up on muse.
Conniving as we are, we offer her up—
all nude and wingless to be judged by the unkind,
and then are puzzled—how did she become
such an evil cobra, sarcastic bitch of venom,
neglecting being beautiful and kind,

which really triggered our interest in her...
So, we discover our innermost mongoose,
partaking in her essence of the snake,
forgetting carelessly that she is still a woman.
And that is where it's time for her to rule:
She gets our book, and hardly thinking twice
she judges harshly, not a drop of pity,
her passion gains the speed of a meteor,
and we are done...
Destroyed by inspiration—
our very own and unencumbered muse,
Such pity that we didn't get to choose
Not really caring for tea and oranges much

Jetlag

That damn coffee was bound to burn—European, redundant, unfinished.
All attempts are futile—half a day had been lost to the moving through
                                                            time zones:
No longer there, but not quite steadily here, as the timing is off,
all connections are grounded solid. The pronouns have cancelled the waltz.
Not all of the comebacks are marked with customs fees,
Lufthansa is always on time, or at least as the schedule merits...

Her voice had a tendency to penetrate the subconscious,
her glance did the same, both were filtered and whispered discomfort.
That song—her guitar could not stand, yet she mulishly had
                                                    it completed—
her wrinkles barely visible, as astrology signs had been carelessly chosen...
That lingering dose undiluted, ambiguous, bordering on acrimony
matched the taste of the coffee, which was never meant to be finished.

The Postscript

The novel is done, while being perpetually shelved,
all drafts are useless, and are therefore forgotten.
The thirst for getting all of the storylines to fly
is getting quenched by the nature of the re-writes.
And there's that ever-present hourglass,
confirming that the time Is so baseless—
when spring is fall, while in the winter—summer's day
is just two hours away as Nemesis is scaling...
The proverbial critic is set with his techniques,
to annihilate the novel at the onset...
His gift for that is getting stale though,
as the manuscript is constantly evolving.
With that the character at center stage
has grounded herself in sad adventures.
Her image still ignites the inspiration,
but contradictory details pour the wine.
The novel itself does remind one of sand,
pristine, as the beginning of a story,
the outcome persists in keeping endings open
in an accomplished and accepted fate

Twin Town in the Middle of the Fields

Gray evening once upon a fall's demise,
no leniency asked for nor expected.
Leaves rustled, taunted by asphalt,
Soprano swiftly bolted from a window,
as if it were not welcome at its source.
I contemplated that particular abode,
as somewhere one could vanish on occasion
to fade in timelessness, among the friendly souls...

We would confide in one another such emotions,
partaking cigarettes and wine in crumbling dorms.
There, the improbable and real ran amok,
and hopelessness was lost to words and music.
Our faces then belonged to ageless paintings
by real artists who had never come to be...
Then I would leave for Evanston again,
where midterms leaned my glance to the skyscrapers
Chicago loomed so vividly and sad...

That fall—what seemed impossible came true,
with her we learned to love and often went to Paris...
As the years passed we grew apart for good,
before our thirties, parted continents and reasons.
And yet that evening in Urbana—on the cusp of fall
was really something that belonged in poems,
and even those few songs we wrote together,
for that alone—my gratitude, Champaign

A Dream

A dream: was reading to my daughter about Ali,
implicitly explaining that the people
with rosaries and turbans kindly greet
their children and their elders —we're all equal.

My wife then let that old teapot to get cold,
while sifting through the foliage, so subtle,
the air of autumn twilight through the fog—
the truth that followed needed no rebuttal.

A dog that ran around calmed and slept
had scores to settle with the nimble squirrels,
the smell of a woman's hair—clean and sweet,
flowed past the clock, forever in deferrals.
A dream

Full Moon Retrospective

In retrospect a June full moon consists
of its half over Jerusalem,
seven-eighths of the one reflecting in Kiev,
and just a fraction of the local one,
which is intentionally flawed,
yet absolutely confident of a win,
while being utterly biased
in its predisposed perception
that all the moonlit ambiences
were not at all present
in the early February twilight,
in which June appeared as a mere remedy
from March inflicted oddities.
That proverbial middle age
is at times susceptible to
metaphors, which appear unfinished
under the influence of full moon fragments,
tangible only from certain heights
where female flight attendants,
while ephemerally smiling,
on occasion spill black coffee
over the top of plastic cups resulting
in the stains on printed matter
of the literary kind,
which initially was published
in a Tel Aviv edition
containing prose written
by the heroine from Kiev,

based on her New York adventures,
whIch she typed in Prague
on a laptop assembled in Reykjavik,
shared with her Manchester lover
over their romantic Miami breakfast...
That was really not a prelude,
but the warmth spread out calmly
over some Northern cities,
of the ones above so mentioned,
and perhaps in others also...
To sum up the full moon essence,
if it may concern throughout—
such a mystic subject matter,
which comes out as unfinished,
hence the flight attendant's movement,
which is mirroring her glances,
she woke up so awfully early,
and got up out of embraces,
dressing swiftly, speeding like crazy,
only to spill the coffee
in the height of many miles
over a magazine reflecting
the full moon inflicted poems...

Canadian Films

I like Canadian films quite a bit, have a real affinity for them.
Nowhere else do they master portraying the understatement
in such an evening glow with just the silhouettes in a soft lighting.
The dialogues there are of an inherent good wine quality.
I am drawn to the way they are able
to show Montreal in predawn twilight,
When the takes of rooftops,
 rain refreshed and subtle, are so real,
as the heroine so impeccably
appears to hear the inner music of her character,
as the urban pastoral floats
unhindered and unassuming over St. Lawrence.
The way they film the sounds of
high heels on the pavement is astonishing.
One could almost feel
the warmth of the residence just left by the character.
There is also that uniquely specific
muted sarcasm often present in the script,
aimed quite amicably at that other large country,
just south of Quebec and Ontario.
And then there is that distinctive respectful adoration
of the character, as a woman,
which is somehow able to avoid all the tired and overused symbolism...
Perhaps, it's the absence of the loud noise
and direct spotlights that makes a difference,
echoing the genuine lyrics of Dassin: *Si tu n'existais* pas...
There is something about Canadian cinema that I cannot quite pinpoint:
Somehow they are able
to visually transmit the ambiance and smell of good coffee,

while the camera lovingly captures the heroine's olive skinned profile
from that Cohen's parable. Then a cut to a window, which is slightly ajar—
that's how Egoyan elects to show
the reflection of a burning candle,
being able to capture
in that reflection the vague ordinariness of the riddle,
following the path to an answer languidly unsweetened...
These films must come from the north of the border.
Such magic is not of Hollywood or even Utah kind.
I like Canadian films quite a bit, have a real affinity for them

* * *

South Florida dreams, heavy rains are all over the coastline.
Coffee makes it all right, as on similar days somewhere else,
Ships are nevertheless braving waves to reach a horizon
and reflecting the skies as in the stained glass of temples erased.
Local winter is such that the rest of the world is in envy,
Yet anomalies here, also present with passing of time
Sea romance is at home when a fog is the imminent standing
frigates and brigantines supersede as if being divine.
Ocean asks for the sky to engage in a round of tango,
interchanging with waltz, when the rhythm slows down a bit
from the memory lane comes the ancient retreat of Palanga,
In the similar rains the subconscious evokes meet and greet.

So awkward back then at the sunset in dunes made of amber,
burning fast was the kiss of a Lithuanian princess my age,
the guitar just took over, as if... In some magical chamber
there was strangeness of guilt—such a sweet adolescence on stage.

This delightful script as if sentenced to moving in circle,
would repeat by the sea, while tempting with colorful scenes:
it was always the muse in a kind of role that would tinkle,
warming me in the rain in the way of the multiple screens.
With a deep gratitude, I indulge in mistrusting the forecast,
winding up at the seaside, where winter could throw you a curve,
at times poems happen instead of the sleep, or in lieu of the breakfast—
love those rains, and the waves, which I am summoned to serve

III

In the City by the Lake

The city by the lake persists—August, evening, light.
It was cold in the morning, revisiting memory lanes,
local winds are as brutal as news spelling out the plight,
best to walk than to drive, that's the only intangible ace.
So peculiar autumn begins, here at times and again,
and the world, by and large does exist in a different realm,
if it rains in the prelude, the thunder is only a matter of when...
Should it pass, will the fear dissipate, preaching desperate calm?
Also August, long ago, somewhere over there,
all the actions and deeds seemed a desperate joke,
as when love had completed its run—full moon in a stare,
May, or June doesn't matter, "the end"—on the pavement in chalk.
Notwithstanding prophecies, all of the words are in vain
dreams, grey hair, enduring the loneliness, being in pain...
Glancing through invisible love at times, just might—
rain would make it feasible—August, evening, light

* * *

*A dedication to the original John Barleycorn Tavern
in Chicago's Lincoln Park, which is no longer...*

—*Se habla Beethoven¿*
—These days, not as often.
Despair of the chapels, the variance of balance.
Street names are the same—so it seems from
Kusturitsa excerpts. Strict grammar is fluid...
Chimeras attached to the sides of the structures
not far from the Luxembourg garden in Paris
glance into the room where the two have just woken
so naked and tired of love that had ended between
its conception and birth, in the winding 90's...
Staccato remains as the sound of Santa Cruz waves,
notwithstanding the empathy gone,
and the echo of: *see you next century, maybe*
That phrase of the eyelids caressing, safe from bad omens.
So many perceptions, akin to those Afghan terrains,
and the poetry lines that are fleeting yet vividly stoic.
At times, all it takes, is a written presumption—
— *Se habla Beethoven¿*

Lincoln Park—Highland Park

All God's Children Can Dance...
—Haruki Murakami

Lincoln Park—Highland Park—
Forty minutes of driving through autumn
on the road that winds, envelops and rings,
as if dancing the salsa along with the leaves
in their timely departure and sudden arrival.
In the line of these cars, so different yet vaguely and
poignantly the same, as if floating in Don Juan's dream,
which was hardly akin to partaking a lesson in waltz,
briefly playing with fate, while melody lasting a lifetime.
From the cars in the queue—all of them but a few,
brass November installing on windshields the sound of rain
with provocative, menacing, savory, delicate samba
it's as if in that saying, "acknowledge the wind
and a cookie will crumble", in translation, however,
it sounds remarkably tired, and even pathetically glib.
There's a reason the dashboard's so bright
when the limit is broken... I am told that it happens
during tango at times, in the midst of milonga,
and in diving as well, when the air is scarce,
way to go is slow, to avoid the proverbial end of the road.
Highland Park—Lincoln Park—
the path is the same, yet significantly shorter,
as the music subsides, it's the voice and guitar of Vysotsky,
that submerge the skyscrapers in a hoarse baritone
of the waning elaborate midnight...
And the air appears to be primed,
all predicaments suddenly over,
and street corners are visibly taken

Feeling California

Sort of feeling California
In a rosin *commeilfaut*...
The destination is set
as if in the issuance of a
power of attorney to Sappho
It is inherently nostalgic for a frequenter
of bookstores and coastal rocks.
The craters of volcanoes are getting cold,
while they were never discovered.
the Atlantic, with its tenderness,
is no match for the Pacific, which is taciturn.
It is getting seismic outside,
The air appears to be trembling.
Quite an intrusive feeling,
certainly worthy of being disproved.
Silence given to the thundering,
nature's absolution is still an option—
it is an absorption of sorts...
California is limited,
it is not for everyone.
Rather similar to the notion
that the spectacle of seeing magic
is reserved for those
who choose to believe in it.
That languishing glance, no longer seductive,
bounces off the wall of reflections,
and all it means really is that
perhaps it's time to read poetry
in California, one day soon

"Fourth in the Count"

The fourth in the count, is January-like this time:
It's piercingly bold, its wind is especially freezing,
and those coffee places,
on side streets, not far from the lake
are offering refuge in the presence of younger poets,
tattooed, and refined.
That calendar spring—
is a stiff global cold consequence,
and the strings of polished and measured rhymes
dueled, as if being artillery rounds, spent and forgotten,
Evanston is so alike and different from its own image of the 80's...
She was the unlikely amalgam of Turkish and Greek in her blood,
a poignant fireball in cold April,
constantly shedding clothes, at times
leaving only her jeans on,
and lighting a cigarette by the dorm window.
She wrote such intense prose,
that reading poetry to her was hopeless.
That one singular coveted word always happens suddenly,
when all the futile efforts to find it are exhausted, similar to the other
early April day long ago,
before the spring final in freshman political science,
which we both aced without really trying,
having slaughtered the night.
Went walking the streets that afternoon,
after the exam—college novices...
We were both born elsewhere,
except that she could fly back to Cyprus anytime,
and I couldn't... My parents were refugees,

leaving the city of my birth forever,
or so it seemed, until the awkward Soviet colossus
fell seemingly overnight.
Once, in Kiev again, a few years ago in April,
as a lawyer and to read poetry as well,
I saw her new novel in the old town bookstore window,
the Ukrainian version of it.
It did not feel surreal,
because once we learned together, not so much
political science... But rather that notion that—
when the fog rolls into Evanston
from Lake Michigan in April,
when all the clothes and pretenses are off,
what remains is the belief that
what you want the most to happen actually does...
Not immediately, and then when it does, it's magic.
Therefore, those coffee places on side streets
in Evanston and Rogers Park,
full of the young and tattooed.
seeking those singular coveted words
are the true windmills of their minds, as April rolls on,
the warmth is inevitable

A Seascape Fragment

Come the pelicans,
by squadron, past the roofs
they screen the ocean,
heading towards the horizon,
where the fog creates mirages
through a geometry of islands,
or brings in the Flying Dutchman,
with its sailors dead and restless,
and its sails that are timeless.

Coastal legends are abundant
with the prose interpretations
of the kind that make the poems
sort of blend and less creative...
Seems alternatively awkward
to suggest that seascape artists
rhyme the images in meter...

Lemon tea goes well with whiskey,
in the moving vivisection
of one's maritime perception,
setting off this pain and tears,
as not all the ships would enter
to the port from the horizon.
Yet, this fatefulness abounds,
unrestricted and vivacious—
which is why that flying squadron
formed by pelicans is doing
mandatory drill flyovers
of the coastal whereabouts

So Starts Manhattan Morning in the Park

Remaining blessed such slow summer days,
when clouds and the fog rejoice embracing
are subjects to the heaven's clay caressing
New York is merely some static in that dance.

Too early for the pavement to be walked
or driven, while languor thus abounds
Comes Central Park... in saxophone and alto sounds
swirling in steam and nacreous in thought.

All those who had exchanged their morning sex
for a nascent spot of nebulous appearance
the heaven's maker deemed to be much less,
and magically dismissed the mystic grievance.

And therefore this place is full of spots,
untouched by time and even spared by weather
where all departures have to do with tether
the music score is reminiscent of the darts.
Such a cloud clad and yet most talented of days,
is mostly odd and out of the order,
yet heaven's maker made it such a border,
and therefore the magic process stays

Mediterranean Self-exile

Self-exile to the Mediterranean waves,
not so much for the sake of aesthetics,
or being astute and clever,
but rather, to break free for a while,
polish off the rhyme a bit and touch that cover,
which casually conceals the grasp of the essence,
an offshoot of truths and routine and
the branching of meanings for the mundane.
It does not offer much hope,
yet contains the sound of eternal preludes,
in which the irrelevance is in the very first octave.

There is that understatement of the summer
in walking on crushed pebbles and those exemplary
couples strolling the *Promenade des Anglais*...
Somehow it comes easier to prose writers—
they cash in the attributes of the plot, and there's the excerpt,
which will be applied, developed and will evolve at some point:
The heroine destined to be absolutely nude,
while the hero, fully clothed and exhaling Gauloises...
Those of us trying to stay within a metered rhyme have it
a bit harsher, as the image we create must be more authentic.

Then this quivering image would be dissected by a critic,
and a self-proclaimed former muse will unequivocally state:
"He is so spent and changing, the whole thing is about me..."
Both of them would be wrong in their assessments of the poem,
in fact, they won't even come close to the original meaning.
For the image in verse is a mere attempt of redemption

for past faults and the spirit of that monstrous blunder,
in which the accidental revenge had never been pleasing,
bringing a wretched discovery that love and friendship
carry faded price tags... They both are but at a few drachmas...

Self-exile to the Mediterranean—
the justifications are superfluous at best...
Then a brief return to Kiev—the surreal realm,
prior to the crossing of the ocean to go home

Snow days in Queens

Long Island in a heavy snowstorm,
all flights at LGA have fallen victims
to cancellations, in a row...—second day.
The parallel of unrelenting blizzard
diagonally also quiet merciless.
These days in Queens, the chain is subtly French,
four stars—that's all of the remaining inventory,
online hotels are hopelessly sold out...
The snow always had its claim to fate.
This city does not rhyme with it at all
that ocean feeling in between the rivers,
so different from the city on the lake,
There always is that year-1984.
It snowed after New Year's, pretty wildly...
Too much in common at eighteen is never good.
Such reminiscences are rare. Must be the snow.
Neither O'Hare, nor Midway are accepting
incoming flights. The blizzard's moving there.
Snow is, perhaps, the only common nuisance
that is unknowingly and nonchalantly shared.

Five from the Past

There is a certain autumn dialogue:
it's part soprano, bit of bass, but mostly whisper
all sort of woven into distant chime,
where tenderness inscribed without words
would not become a parable or canon.

They came towards the doorbell and it rang,
a door then opened—while shadows hovered over
the wine was sparkling, as were the certain words,
without meddling, just echoed in the music
As evening neared, they departed. Strangers still.

Not so much out of disbelief,
but rather for a reason that is doubtful,
while yet the overwhelming Babylon
seemed so indifferent to the anomaly transpiring,
all that remained was to believe, and then forget.

How inappropriate—a prisoner prevailed,
she won, her argument was raw and overwhelming:
dark eyes and raven hair—all in place.
The court had granted total absolution
and then still waited for her nudity to come.

Rains reign supreme over the capital of France,
or so they should, according to the forecast,
but it's a sham, it's really warm and dry—
in times like these, not missing the Midwest,
one happily forgets the snows of Russia

85

Lake Effect

The lake effect:
—A special kind of genre,
when through a veil of incoming mist,
so masterful in vanishing abruptly,
that there is no horizon, and no railing,
as, when indeed, there is no longer you,
but yet, at random you proceed eastbound...
The lake effect, persists in Kiev still,
so far from here, that one is left to ponder:
Is it for real, the Vozdvizhenka[1] as such?
Or those are truly just the dreamy remnants
of courage momentarily acquired,
which dissipated with the affirmation,
how truly far away it is from here...

The lake effect, as if a shrapnel piece
of winter, so local and suburban
that it is tortured by proverbial self-pity,
not being able to define itself,
its chartered path, which had become inherent
in all those years when forecasting ran afoul.
This juncture of discovery and timing,
when local Indians gave up without a fight.
Well, practically... Of course, there was betrayal,
but over all, there wasn't that much blood.

---

[1] A historic neighborhood in central Kiev.

The lake effect, despite the cozy warmth,
nevertheless, demands an open air,
which is no longer primed by the guitar,
but rather with a mountain of a sky
so thickly kneaded in the entourage of mixes
as if it is about to succumb
to the temptation of a certain painting
that glorifies the epical demise...
And what would follow is a period of myth,
with extraordinary happenings occurring,
being explained monotonously with
such boring formulas and not so perfect grammar,
inherent in their printed postulates...
The lake effect, so pure and non-verbose,
that any words would miserably fail,
especially in Russian, from the heart

Northbound

The flight takes off from Fort Lauderdale,
glides across the air, and heads inevitably North,
presenting a chance to separate
the grain from the chaff, through the sky dash.
From all the chatter prior to that takeoff,
the bottom line is rather trite—
the northbound route is a mere penalty
for that seeming ease of triumphs past.
The glance below confirms the fact,
that there is still
a certain Confederacy, below the wings,
which begs the thought—of yet another place,
where holding on to wealth is oddly wasted—
dear leader will make sure of proper ways to take it all,
and then some in the process.
And if that chain of seemingly coincidental occurrences
presumes a lucky break, or similar anomaly,
it's worth remembering that
the Apaches were the nobility of the prairies...
However, all of the above lines merely stray
from the originally invented cinematic script:
A summer night in Havana, where
she is obviously sleeping as she does, since it's hot,
a spider crawls on the wall...
None of that nonsense would transpire in the North,
where folks proudly sport many clothing layers
under the brands of "The North Face"...
In the North, there is only
blatant and undoubted common sense,

there's no wistful nonsense,
as was so eloquently noted in no uncertain terms
by a past muse turned harsh but fair literary critic.
Fair enough, if only the script writer
did not know her so well,
so as an accolade to the dubious pleasures of the past,
he offered no defense of the original...
Still, that's not what the piece is about,
all these detours are sadly misleading,
and there is that obvious factor in the plot,
which snowballs in the morning—typical for the North.
The North persists in merciless winds
and the rest of its abusing, unbearable weather,
which only accentuates the outcome,
being nonsensical and blurred as an indy feature should be

An Afterthought

Foretelling at times is not worth that proverbial penny, distressed,
when it comes as a rule, takers are but a few to reflect on the meaning,
it's akin to philosophy musings in various state of undress,
that tremendously subtle, but such a superfluous feeling.

When the tea is getting cold, and reality scolds the edge
of the grammar-related subjunctive case, so remarkably tilted,
what matters is not the memory of the scene on that theater stage,
but rather the part of the play, which left everybody bewildered.

Without the close-up of the faded angle—to the top of her breasts,
then cut to the shoulder blades, as she slowly steps into the circle,
the audience gasps and the image most certainly lingers and lasts,
long after the drop of the curtain, which tends to be bluish and purple.

There will be countless flowers, backstage and in dressing rooms,
standing ovations, jubilant press in Tokyo, Paris, Manhattan, London,
however, she would much rather do voice-over in full feature cartoons,
if only they could come home together, she is so tired of being stronger

"Tall Ships Arriving"

Tall ships arriving in the city by the lake—
the *Iliad* enumeration has been slowed.
The winds have calmed, the warmth returned instead
and certain magic from the fog appeared and flowed.
So fleeting, nonchalant, seemingly light
the night approached as if a dazed Venetian beauty,
the feeling similar to an ascending flight
conquering clouds, matter-of-factly, not out of duty.
Then further up—all prophecies aside,
as things transpire, often hurting in the process
the signs celestial, to be approached in stride,
as theory would have it on Parnassus...

That early August with arrival of the ships,
the outlook appeared so daringly unlikely,
what follows scripts that were composed like this
are gypsy tales, thus they are slanted slightly.
That fairway of convoluted fate,
not underscored, or given in italics,
is so impractical and needs a gutted slate,
no use in fighting it, when colors fade metallics.
Then, what takes over is that certain might,
so overwhelming to the eyes and vital senses,
that one would think that the resulting plight,
involves the ships in all its vast circumstances...
Tall ships arriving

The Ocean Bridge

The end of the 70's. September. Kiev. Soviet Ukraine.
I was still there, among my classmates at a celebration:
The table was set, and our drink of choice was "Buratino lemonade",
a picture perfect fête from all possible angles,
a real pre-teen party in the capital on the Dnieper river.
Only the chosen ones were invited, a serious contingent, indeed:
most of us were dressed in fashionable garb of the local outlet,
except the birthday man—Andrey, he looked strangely all-American,—
his émigré aunt in Philadelphia, sent clothing parcels.
It was a big secret though, such was the order of things in the USSR,
but when you're ten, your thoughts are not of that—
but mostly about being seriously behind on the math homework,
and damn, how could *Dinamo Kiev* not score
against that lousy team from small French town of *Saint-Etienne*.
Meanwhile the birthday man was blushing—
the beauty of the class had raised her "Buratino" glass,
while it's true that we were not yet of age,
her passion could only be held back with tears even then.
We made it though, the toast had gone all right.
The gifts of bubble gum from Poland were proudly presented,
We were all ten years old—which really meant a lot
to our still being unaware how small and peculiar this planet is.

I wasn't at the celebration of his twentieth, alas,
We all had reasons various and different.
There was a war. My rights were not predicted
descriptions of the pain are never right.
Oh yes, that war has passed through me as well,
My inner *Salang* too required courage,

even though mind readers and magicians
kept on insisting that I shouldn't bother with parallels.
I wouldn't be able to hold the siege for days, most likely
as did his Soviet garrison of Host in the Afghan mountains,
and as did the American garrisons a mere two decades later and still...
My inner airfield, of course, had seen its share of crashes,
My lines remained, I've let imagination
see his twentieth—on mountain road, they've opened
a never-ending bottle of the local moonshine, and through the miles
I heard in Russian:—"We remain alive somehow..."
That day I couldn't light a cigarette in the wind
between the walls of my beloved alma-mater,
and my Greek girlfriend said: Not easy, being American, huh?—
have some vodka in honor of your friends from the past...

A bit later, on the left bank of the Seine,
a Romanian refugee offered to read some tarot cards.
"Forget about them"—she said—
"that one Andrey, is missing in action.
What's a childhood friendship in the realm of the universe, anyway..."

In 1991, a few months before the Soviet Union ceased to be
I landed in Moscow for the first time as an American.
Dialing a 70's phone number,
I sensed indifference on the other end, as the phone kept on ringing.
My friends, the Moscow theater elite, whom I met in the States didn't care.
I kept on dialing the number, this time from a place in Kiev,
perhaps my sense of reality had gone astray...
Suddenly a woman's voice answered and said solemnly—"Andrey is gone..."
—...But he'll be back in an hour, they've taken their daughter to the toy fair..."

We drank a strangely canned vodka, and it tasted sweet.
It was raining in Kiev... Some people stood nearby.
He was taking his wife and daughter to Leningrad in the morning,
My wife and I were flying home to Chicago,
with a stopover in Paris in a day.
We didn't talk of how my family left that city of ours for good,
never to return,

or how he was dying
in the hall of the Kabul hospital just a few years ago,
having been helicoptered in from an ambush on the mountain overpass...
...And that he survived, again somehow,
because another classmate of ours
was a temporarily visiting surgeon there,
and got him on a table to operate on...
We will be convinced time and again that coincidences matter...

I keep coming back to my City,
eternalized and capitalized by Bulgakov.
I cannot imagine not being able to...
Not walking its streets, and not sitting
at a set table in the same apartment,
where we celebrated his 10th birthday.
Pretty much the same people are around that table,
the same "chosen ones" as in 1977.
Our beautiful women classmates, and men,
much older looking than we should be.
We celebrated his 30th there, as the century was ending,
and his 50th, just recently.
I can't tell him, or the other classmates of ours,
that I am really glad that they were
turned away by the Ukrainian Army
from applying to go to the front when Russia attacked.
The same coincidences rule:
They were spared from perishing in hopeless Donbass battles.
We all are helping out otherwise in the military hospitals,
and by other means, as we can...
Our city street, where our school still is
and where Andrey's and my old apartments are
was recently renamed.
It now boasts the name of Senator McCain,
instead of the Soviet war hero...
We don't talk about that much. Would probably disagree.
I just keep hoping that the coincidences last,
and that our Bridge over the Ocean stays

Snow and Fog of the January Kind

The snow and fog, such January quirks
within the city by the lake, in ancient prairies
it doesn't matter when and if one speaks.
as lack of faith in its abundance varies.

Here, one may vanish, having chosen not to light
the cigarette, that wind would promptly shutter,
then while staring at the breathing bay, not quit...
Learn perseverance, which is proper.

Here women year round wearing boots,
as if the war is nearby, and breathing fire
sweaters and nothing underneath, they also choose,
ignoring more appropriate attire.

And while relatively north to the Gulfstream,
it's sort of west to the appearance of New Yorkers
to Californians, it is the eastern beam,
yet south of Montreal on summer scorchers.

This place is much inherent in the craft
outside of rhymes, acidic words and crude ellipses,
we ended up here, finishing the draft,
belonging elsewhere, as was prophesied by gypsies

SERGEY ELKIN

A Conversation with Gari Light

Summer 2018

Gari Light is largely rooted in Chicago, albeit sometimes with sojourns of various length to New England, Europe, Florida, Washington and other places... He is a lawyer with many years of domestic and international business practice, as well as the area of human rights. However, if jurisprudence is his profession, poetry is his calling. He has been polishing his skills in this realm since his early adolescence. Having published widely in literary periodicals throughout the world, he also has several poetry books out. His recent collection of poems, "Trajectories of Returns," was awarded the Literary Prize of the Ukraine's Writers' Union. Here are several excerpts from an interview done recently for the Reklamamedia, a social portal.

Gari, you were born in Kiev, a capital of Ukraine which was still part of the Soviet Union at the time, as you write in one of your poems, "a year before the tanks in Prague..." What do you remember today about your childhood in Kiev?

As for my personal, brighter childhood recollections of Kiev in the 70's in the time's refraction—are mostly the good things—my parents' great book collection, which I only began discovering at the time. Also the usual things: playing non-stop soccer and street hockey in the courtyard until dark with friends. Discovering the inspiration of blooming spring chestnuts and lilacs in the great Botanical garden with an incredible view of the Vydubetsky monastery. In the summer the joys of the beaches of the Dnieper and Desna. And of course, the amazing recollections of absolutely magical winter snowfalls... I also recall that time being implicitly riddled with literary images. Kiev is a large, yet very compact and warm city, with a particular southern touch, not at all imperial, as say Moscow and Leningrad were... Actually—it is still very much my city. I started coming back there as soon as the Soviet Union collapsed. Of course, much has changed there, but my returns there are not at all nostalgic rather—to me they are organically necessary. I have good friends who still live there. They are dear to me, as well as the City itself. Tragically, there is also the never-ending notion, the genetic memory of Holocaust. My grandparents managed to leave on almost next to last trains with my parents as babies, before the Soviets abandoned Kiev to the Nazis in the fall of 1941. Everyone from our family who stayed, were murdered in the ravines of Babiy Yar... In the most recent few years I have been coming to Kiev in the fall, spending long hours standing over those ravines. There is a feeling over there that fate, time, and human nature are all very relative concepts...

Even though I often recall the time before leaving the Soviet Union in 1979, in a somewhat skewed retro sepia color, I have no illusions about that period at all. By that time, the Soviet government had moved away from the Stalinist enthusiasm for praising and making heroes of executioners. Yet, I still recall that even in our relatively progressive school in the city center, there was definite profound presence of Communist ideology, and occasional instances of state supported antisemitism. As you noted in that quote from a poem—my childhood did correspond with the time soon after the Soviet tanks were on the streets of Prague, the decade before that—they literally drowned in blood the Hungarian uprising in Budapest, and virtually that month of our departure, in December of 1979, the Soviets invaded Afghanistan. It seems that the bitter lessons of the past were not learned by those who today decide to send

Russian soldiers, to die in foreign lands. Today, the same tanks with virtually the same insignia on their armor burn in the distant Syrian provinces and steppes of the Ukrainian Donbass...

Do you remember your first poem?

I recall that it was somehow related to our family cat—Bahira, in Kiev. I tried rhyming something in connection to her. Was probably fascinated with observing her habits. I was always very fond of felines. Cats are very intelligent beings, and with those lucky humans, whom they consider worthy on some scale of their own, they communicate on equal terms without servility... As for other attempts at rhyming—I recall that a bit later, I almost consciously wrote down some lines, while temporarily living in Ladispoli, an Italian seaside suburb of Rome, where we were waiting for paperwork during the immigration process in coming to America. I was already about twelve years old, and I realized that something incomprehensible was happening to me: some lines appeared as if being dictated, and I did not know what to do with them. So, I wrote them down.

Did you ever think that you would become a poet?

Of course not. At the age of thirteen or fourteen I recall writing a short story, which involved some romantic science fiction of sorts. It was even marginally popular among my school friends, especially girls, mostly for including that romantic part. That was already here, on Chicago's Northside. I continued to rhyme some lines all along, but would have never dared to call those poetry for a long time. I also recall writing more short stories in the 80's. After I realized that writing is not a passing phase for me, but is something much more important, I started approaching it with a certain discipline. Always tried to keep reading good poetry and prose, both classical and contemporary. That's the only real way to learn. On and off for about twenty years now, I've been working on something that may be attributed to the genre of a large novel. The canvas of that scheme are constantly evolving... I think sometime in the near future, I may consider publishing some fragments from it, and see where it takes me... Regarding the title of the poet which you mentioned... Through the years of being in the literary circles, I've noticed that many folks today think of themselves in those terms without giving it much thought. I completely agree with the legendary Canadian poet Leonard Cohen, who has repeatedly said that being called "a poet" is actually a title, a designation that is better assessed from the outside. When the established and universally respected writers of previous generations as well as my visibly gifted literary contemporaries characterize me in this way, I am grateful to them, and much humbled. However, I hope, that literary experience is a life-long learning process. Indeed, a considerable part of my time is connected with poetry. Several books have been published on both sides of the Atlantic. I sincerely believe that I am at least following the course.

Where do you see the connection between jurisprudence and poetry?

I began to ponder on that while still being in law school. It seems to me that creativity should always have a place in the lawyer's craft. While poetry, in turn, is by no means solely involves momentary improvisation of inspiration. The muse of poetry Erato—is quite a serious lady, who does not always prefer creative chaos. In my opinion, she is impressed by the presence of a certain respectable pattern. On the other hand, I always try to introduce an element of creativity into my legal practice, including during my (formerly frequent) court appearances. When, while following the procedure, you on occasion go beyond some kind of predictability—this at times could be very useful for achieving a desired outcome.

I'll ask more broadly: what is the circle of your favorite poets?

I'm afraid my answer will not be too original." It is clear, that those of us who were born in the former Soviet Union are all initially fascinated with the poems of Pushkin and Lermontov. This being the interview format, it is perhaps not the right time and place for me to present a long list of Russian, English, American, as well as French and Spanish poets who have become important to me (p.100) in my American youth and during the university years. There were many. I could tell you, though, who's poetry volumes are constantly on my favorite proverbial book shelf, literary within momentary reach, not in alphabetical or any other order: Elizabeth Bishop, Anna Akhmatova, Joseph Brodsky, Alexander Pushkin, Ridyard Kipling, Gabriel Garcia Lorca, Boris Pasternak, Andrei Voznesensky, Leonard Cohen, W.H. Auden Czeslaw Milosz, Andrei Codrescu and Vladimir Vysotsky... There are many more but these are certainly the ones.

Did English become your language?

Of course, it did. This is the main language of my country, in which I have been living for nearly forty years. This is the language of my profession, as well as the language of several of the world's greatest literatures. Naturally, I cannot call American English my native language, but I must admit that sometimes it is easier for me to formulate some thoughts in English than in Russian. Russian is my first language, acquired at birth in the always bilingual Kiev. In its multilingualism Kiev, it is akin to Montreal and Tel Aviv. I am glad that I did not lose the native command of Russian, and almost native command of Ukrainian for many years of the physical separation from the habitat of those languages, which could very well have happened. Does happen often to the children of first generation immigrants. It is a natural process. Nothing wrong with it. I just got lucky, not to have that happen to me. I do not believe that any particular country has an exclusive claim on the language. Russian is an amazing language, which was never the property of Stalin's Soviet Union, and similarly would never be a property of Putin's Russia, as much as some folks over there, and even here might wish that being a case. Vladimir Nabokov proved that view wrong once and for all. In general, that whole notion of languages is interesting: in the not so distant past, mastery of several major languages was perfectly in the order of things. I think this is still the case in Europe... For the first seven years of my life, I spent a lot of time in my grandparents' Kiev apartment, where they spoke Yiddish to each other. It is a somewhat sad mystery to me, as to why I did not acquire that language (with the exception of a few words and phrases). Recently, in New York, I visited an interesting literary event of the *Vremena* literary magazine, where I serve on the editorial board. At that event, the world-famous pianist Evgeny Kissin read his poems in Yiddish, which he learned to perfection and from scratch. It was truly fascinating. I would also really like to someday return to Yiddish, and also learn Hebrew. It seems to me extremely important to know the history and language of our ancestors.

Is the Ukrainian language included in the list of your languages?
Of course, like it should be for any Kievite by birth. I understand absolutely everything in that language and speak Ukrainian fairly well. True, not as good as in Russian and in English... I am glad that my poems were translated into Ukrainian, I hope to master it further in the future.

Living in Chicago, don't you sometimes have the feeling that you live on the outskirts, sensing a certain provinciality of the place?
In no way should anybody ever consider Chicago a literary province, or any province at all. It is not! We live in a world class, top of the line metropolis. Hemingway was born here. Saul Bellow, Theodore Dreiser, Carl Sandberg, Philip Roth, all had

lived and wrote their famous works in Chicago. Scott Turrow works and writes his best-selling books here. I am sure that in this format I, unfortunately, did not mention all of the literary talent with Chicago connections. Let's also not lose sight of the fact that Chicago is a city of diasporas. When I visit local literary events and talk with writers who, while being based here write in Spanish, Polish, the Balkan languages, I certainly would not exclude a possibility that the next Gabriel Garcia Marquez or Jorge Luis Borges could now live in Pilsen, while the heirs to the traditions of Stanislav Lem and Ezhi Letz may well dwell in Vicker Park, while the new Milorad Pavic and Milan Kundera— could very well be currently drawing their inspiration from the promenades of Lincoln Park.

Your latest collection of poems entitled Return Trajectories, was recently awarded the literary prize of Ukraine's Writers' Union. As far as I understand, certain geographical spots are important to you. Kiev and Chicago—by definition. What other cities and places are included in this realm? What do you plan to do next?

The Ushakov Literary Prize—has been in existence for many years. It is the iconic prize of the Ukraine's Writers' Union. Honestly, it was a very pleasant surprise for me. I am honored and very humbled to be in the company of outstanding writers, who became laureates of this award in the past. *Return Trajectories* became a very important stepping stone in my development as an author. While that book contains a symbiosis of selected poetry from my previous books, it also includes a significant number of new poems written in a different reality. I mean the time period which began transpiring worldwide in 2014, and certainly entered into the path of appearing surreal after 2016. It seems to me, that we now may be witnessing a somewhat pivoting round of civilization's existence. The book's content in various ways is connected to places, where I do not feel as a stranger at all, despite the rapidly changing world. Of course, it is Chicago and Kiev, first and foremost. But also—Miami, New York, London, Prague and Paris, among others. The next step for me is, hopefully a book of poems in English, which I have been working on for a long time now. I am hoping that celestial bodies could align in a certain way, and that book, which, I think will have a symbolic, water-related title, would become a reality sometime soon.

A Moscow-based poet Maria Stepanova told me recently that there is currently a boom in poetry readings over there. Do you think the situation in Chicago is somewhat different?

It is my observation, which some people may disagree with—that poetry even when it steps out from the intended and preferred pedestal of a one-on-one interaction between a reader and a writer in the realm of a book, still largely remains a chamber experience, a revelation of sorts. It involves the necessity of an exchange between poets reading out loud and listeners who are able to immediately comprehend the meaning. This is not easy. The presence of attentive and critically thinking people at a poetry event, is key to any successful reading. Those times, when entire stadiums in Moscow, and other cities world-wide were gathering huge crowds for poetry events are long gone, along with the legendary poets and overall cosmic realities, which were all of the phenomenon of the fantastic decade in the 60's. Having said that – there are still plenty of fine, more intimate venues in New York, Chicago, Seattle as well as other American cities, where the ambiance of a genuine poetry reading is still very much a norm. Also, in our peculiar times, it turned out that literature is quite comfortable being based on the Internet. This is neither good nor bad— it is a reality. I will gladly believe Maria, that people are happy to attend literary events in Moscow. I would not know. I stopped going to Moscow a long time ago. As a listener and as an author, I've witnessed wonderful audiences at literary evenings in Kiev. People read, and this is the most important thing nowadays. It seems to me that the current time is perfect to catch upon reading and re-reading Chekhov, Hemingway, Faulkner, Vonnegut, other classics, as well as high-quality modern literature. Now, as never before, the time has come to read, so that in two or three years we can all, as in the good old days, without interrupting each other, discuss what we read over the years when confrontation and divide will cease ruling the agenda. Reading good books now would, hopefully help us to regain some civility and find a common language in the future. For a few years and counting now, I deliberately have not participated in politically-related conversations and discussions. These discussions now lead to nothing but one outcome: People who used to be otherwise close, cease communicating with each other. As for strangers, where there used to be a place for a dialogue just a short time ago, in today's reality such dialogue does not exist. People stopped hearing each other. A this point in time you simply cannot convince strangers of anything. It is a waste of time—yours and theirs. I sincerely believe that we will begin to hear and understand each other again, perhaps in a few years, although I would really like it to happen sooner. In the meantime, in my opinion, it is a high time to read good books. Perhaps those books could serve as natural proverbial ice breakers and conversation starters, when we are ready to talk, while actually hearing each other again.

GARI LIGHT

A Biographical Note

Born in Kiev, Ukraine in 1967. Lives in the United States since 1980.
Graduated from Northwestern University with Departmental
Honors B. A. in Slavic Literatures Studies in 1989. Became a lawyer
some short time after, and worked in the area of international
jurisprudence, both in the U.S, and abroad. Since 1993, Gari's
poetry is published regularly in the literary journals and poetry
anthologies of the United States, Canada, Israel, Europe and
Ukraine. He is a member of the American PEN Center and the
Writer's Union of Ukraine. Light's several books of poetry were
published in Russian, starting in 1992. The most recent collection,
entitled *The Return Trajectories* has been published simultaneously
in the U.S. and Ukraine in 2017. It was awarded the Ukrainian
Writers Union's Literary Prize for the best collection of original
poetry published that year. Gari regularly takes part in poetry
readings and other literary events on both sides of the Atlantic.

The author is genuinely grateful to his friends and those
with whom he has vital common denominators...
Those who are virtually owed for the confluence
that occurred so naturally with the abodes
of their souls on the shores of Lake Michigan,
Desna and Dnieper rivers, as well as those
of Yarkon River and Neva...
The deltas of Hudson and East River,
Mississippi and the Gulf...
Both shores of the Atlantic, the Canadian
and American side of the Pacific...
Confluences would otherwise be incomplete.

ACKNOWLEDGEMENTS

Throughout the years I have been honored with publications in various literary journals worldwide. While I may not be able to list all of them here, I am especially grateful to the following:

The Jerusalem Review (Israel) and its editor Igor Byalsky;
The New Review (New York) and its editor Marina Adamovich;
The Coast, (Philadelphia) and its editor Igor Mikhalevich--Kaplan;
Vremena (New York) and its editor David Guy;
Novy Svet (Toronto, Canada) and its editor Alena Joukova;
Etazhi (Boston–Moscow) and its editors Irina Terra and Igor Kuras;
Kreschatik (Germany–Ukraine) and its editor Boris Markovsky;
The New Continent (Chicago) and its editor Igor Tsesarski.

While working on *Confluences*, I was fortunate to read some of the materials in the book at various Chicago-area, and greater Miami literary venues, which are run by the known and talented people. In that regard, my most sincere gratitude to:

Poetry Night at the Outdoor Café Reading Series and its curators Jenene Ravesloot and Tom Roby IV;
Rhino Reads at the Bookends and Beginnings, and Rhino editors Ralph Hamilton and John McCarthy;
After Hours Reading Series and Albert DeGenova;
Albany Park Library Readings and its curator Jerry Pendergast;
Sunny Isles Library Reading Series, branch manager Hector Vasquez and librarian Faina Akhinblit;
Highland Park Poetry and Jennifer Dotson.

I would like to thank Tatiana Retivov for her encouragement of this publication, masterful editing and writing a Forward to *Confluences*.

Many thanks to my long-time friend, a wonderful, talented writer, and an amazing publisher Simon Kaminski, whose professionalism and sheer dedication to the printed word would never cease to amaze me.

I am especially grateful to my good friend from the New Jersey side of the Hudson river Misha Mazel—a genuine poet, artist and the Internet guru, for his valuable advice and inexhaustible optimism.

I would like to thank all of my talented poet friends who took the time to read my poems and write kind and thoughtful reflections, which are indispensably integral to the fate of this book.

My special thanks to the true master of poetry—Lennart Lundh. His perception on what this book is about, quite precisely defined and captured its essence.

My endless gratitude to the magically talented poet Tinker Greene. While reading his poetry at the Newberry library one day this past summer, I finally decided that *Confluences* should no longer be put on the back burner, and that I would at least try to seek his guidance in that regard. Since then, I had the privilege to translate the poetry of Mr. Greene, as well as read along with him at the aforementioned Outdoor Café Literary Series. Not only did I have the honor of receiving his masterful guidance on *Confluences*, but it was Tinker's direct involvement in thoroughly reading the manuscript during the various stages of its development, which actually made this book a reality. I am humbled and grateful.

"Well into his third decade as a poet, Light uses his mature voice in Confluences to translate multicultural images and locales. These are truly love poems and war songs crafted as universal encounters on those battlefields."
—*Lennart Lundh*, author of *The River Singing*,
Workhorse, 2019

"*Beautiful poems by Gari Light, who writes poems both in Russian and in English. These English poems by Gari have the same energy and elegance as his Russian poems, and they are enriched by his multilayered, polyphonic use of the English language to express thoughts and feelings with sophistication and humor.*"
—*Nina Kossman*, editor of the anthology
Gods and Mortals: Modern Poems on Classical Myths,
Oxford University Press, 2001

"*Gari Light's English-language debut poetry collection features meditative, streams-of-consciousness prose poems in free verse, a deviation from his strictly metered Russian poetry. Confluences—the meeting points of experiences put together... These poems are like seascapes, or better yet dreamscapes, sweeping the reader into a swirl.*"
—*Stella Hayes*, author of *One Strange Country*,
What Books Press, 2020

"*To read Gari Light's poetry is to take a journey to far-flung places: Ukraine, Prague, the ravines of Babi Yar, Jerusalem, Chicago, Leonard Cohen's New York City apartment and, even, into the atmosphere, 35 miles above the earth, looking down at the Hudson Valley. So evocative is the poet's language, so affecting are his deeply felt emotions, that the reader feels invited to take a piece of each place as a keepsake or talisman; so as to forget neither the beauty nor the horror of it all.*"
—*David Silverman*, author of *And God Created Hummus*,
Glass Lyre Press, 2019

"At last we have collected in print the first poems in English of my trilingual friend and fellow inhabitant of our "city by the lake": urbane ruminations in graceful verse. Specific places are invoked—Miami, Prague, Flushing Meadows, Venice, Greece, Paris, Montreal, Kiev, various unnamed bodies of water—but our author is "belonging elsewhere," often enough 30,000 feet up, peering out of a tiny circular window at a distant cloudy world infused with wistful memory and tender regret. Inevitably it is autumn, with steady rain and the hiss of distant tires. Gratefully we warm ourselves at the hearth of our poet's eloquent and complex music."

—*Tinker Greene*, author of *Blue Flame Ring*,
A forthcoming poetry collection

"Reading Gari Light's poetry myself, and hearing him read it to the audience, I discerned in his dynamic, and often sardonic texts that certain note of melancholy, that thoughtful sadness, without which a set of merely metered lines may not be deemed real poetry… Gari appears to be longing for that proverbially fleeting peace of mind, in that one and only spot, where there is priceless inner calm. It's that peace of mind, that was so coveted by another Kievite, who had also left the city of his birth, but who for himself, and for millions of others capitalized it into being known as the City."

— *Alexei Nikitin*, author of *Y.T. [Istemi]*,
Melville House, 2016

"The poetry of Gary Light is not just multidimensional in a way we usually deem the meaning of that word… This author's poetry is so familiar with the fifth dimension that it easily takes the reader beyond the boundaries, into the sixth, seventh and God knows which other dimensions. His words delicately embrace, tactfully envelop in fog, then dissolve into the twilight and easily relocate from the City on the Lake to the City on the River, from childhood to adulthood, from reality to a dream—and vice versa. But the most important advantage of these verses is that they have a special magic—the magic of humanity."

—*Liya Chernyakova*, author of *Naked Words*,
Bagriy & Company, 2016

"To comprehend one's place at the break of continents, beliefs and homelands—is incredibly complex. To do so with taste, keeping within the boundaries of style, with that certain sensation of the realm of sound—only a few are capable of doing that... And that is how I perceive the poetry being created by Gari Light."

—**Dmitriy Kimelfeld**, poet and songwriter,
Jerusalem

"Geography does play a significant role in any real poet's work. That particular urge to keep moving contributes to a certain creative energy. Gari Light does move around quite a bit, which is evident from geographical particulars present in his poetry—Ladispoli, Tarusa, Kiev, Moscow, Trakai, Koktebel, Florida, Chicago, New York... I assume, quite a few experiences, which were encountered by the author at those locales transformed into poetry lines. I would also venture a guess, that had Gari been born some three decades earlier, he would feel right at home in the literary tradition of the 60's. It seems that the notions of his soul, as well as his moral stands are much in line with those wonderful times."

—**David Guy**, editor-in-chief of
Vremena Literary Review,
New York

"Within his poetry Gari Light corresponds with the past, the present and the future, openly and without any pretense, doing so with a certain veiled sadness, through the looking glass of his own time, that genuine American Kievite, with an exquisite style of his own..."

—**Vasyl Drobot**, poet,
Kyiv

Made in the USA
Middletown, DE
18 September 2022